The Wrap-up Years

Life is made up of decisions—
some of them major ones . . .
perhaps the most shattering
is to give up a portion
of one's independence . . .

We couldn't have made a better choice!

The Wrap-up Years

by
Clara Verner

Beacon Hill Press of Kansas City
Kansas City, Missouri

Copyright 1982
By Beacon Hill Press of Kansas City

ISBN: 0-8341-0799-6

Printed in the
United States of America

Cover by: Royce Ratcliff

Appreciation

is herewith expressed to the following:

my daughter, Mariana Eckel, for her idea of the questionnaire;

Jane Meyer, a fellow resident, for her thought of the chapter on contentment and for her much typing;

Doris Mann, former president of the NWMS of the Arizona District;

and Rev. McIntosh, pastor of the Church of the Nazarene of Prescott;

for their kindness in reading and evaluating the manuscript;

and, last but not least, to my husband, Thomas Everett Verner, for his never-ending thoughtful cooperation.

This treatise is dedicated to a successful singer whose highest acclaim has been as an evangelistic choir director, musician, and composer; who is now recognizing the approach of the wrap-up years and wished for a discussion of the subject:

Ron Lush

Contents

1

The Wrap-up Years*

Well, well! Old age has finally caught up!

What is old age? My mother died at 72, my father at 86. Tom's father died at 80, his stepmother at 80, and his mother at 35 of typhoid fever. My maternal grandparents both died at 76, though several years apart. We are now in our 80s, so it seems natural for us to think of 80 as old. However, here at the home where we live, 80 is almost average. There are a few less than that, but many, many are older. We even have two centenarians! One is in the infirmary, but the other is up and around. Both are clear in their thinking, but the second one is still caring for her person and is active, even getting to church almost every Sunday.

When you associate daily with people from 89 to 100 who are alert and sharp, 80 seems young. How come we are in a home, at this age?

The rule here is that if you are not ambulatory when you arrive, you don't enter. Many homes are like that. More than one couple has said, "Oh, not yet! Maybe next

---

*A phrase coined by Dr. Robert Schuller; used by permission.

year!" Then a heart attack or some other illness strikes, and the opportunity is gone.

People dread going to an institution. Once upon a time, "homes" were only for people too poor to go anywhere else; or for those whose children did not want to be bothered and deliberately "dumped" them. Not so any more. Now people up in years *choose* institutional living. People live longer if they don't have to crowd in with a family of lively young children who must have all the first attention of the adults. The elderly more often than not require special diets, a nuisance in family living. And living alone in old age can be both lonely and risky.

In a good home, medical attention is at hand every week and oftener when needed. The nurses make certain weekly checks and are alert to detect any change which needs the doctor's immediate attention. The meals are regular and prompt. One woman who went away to visit relatives said when she returned, "It's surely nice to get back to regular meals. Where I was, we had breakfast at eight or nine o'clock, and supper so late in the evening that I was sleepy and wanted to go to bed. They were wonderful to me and I was happy to be with them, but I surely am glad to be home!"

Some of us have another problem. The rigid regularity of meals is one of the adjustments we have to make. We can't sleep in, as we often did before we came. We can't snack all the time, either. But it is also amazing to see how much the regularity and dieting do for the body. We are, for the most part, in much better health than when going our own careless ways.

No one skips meals because of the blues! Attendance at meals is a requirement. If a resident is not at the table, a nurse goes to the room to investigate. If the resident is ill, a wheelchair is produced and the patient is taken to the infirmary. Moral: If you don't want to go to the infirmary, you get yourself to the dining room! It reminds me of childhood days when "sick" was an excuse to keep from going to school—and immediately Mother produced a dose of castor oil!

There is much to be said for a good "home." Here the heavy laundry is done for us, although we have equipment for doing our personal laundry. The rooms are mopped once a week, and we don't have to do that. Another person cleans the bathrooms once a week. With no dishes to wash and no meals to shop for and prepare, we have plenty of time to do some of the things we used to just dream of doing.

Life is made up of decisions—some of them major ones, many requiring a great deal of thought and prayer. Of these, perhaps the most shattering to the emotions is the decision to give up a portion of one's independence to enter such an institution.

Our family, like so many others in America, had scattered. We were hundreds of miles away from most of our loved ones. Our telephones were used often, so we did not feel too far away, and we had few health problems; therefore, we didn't see each other more than once a year. As time went by, our friends became our family, in a way.

We didn't realize how much older we were getting, for we were busy making a living, and didn't need much care —or so we thought. Suddenly I was hospitalized. The daughter who lived nearest was alerted and came at once. When things became too heavy for her, the second daughter, who had no children, flew in and lent a hand. The third daughter kept in touch.

This crisis passed, but before long I was back in the hospital! The nearest daughter came, and a neighbor insisted on helping, too. This pricked my pride as she had a big family of her own. I didn't like to impose on her, so the second daughter came back.

It was time to make some changes. A lot of discussion followed and, in the end, we sold our home. We gave the second daughter power of attorney to handle our affairs if or whenever we might be unable to do it.

Having sold our home, we moved to Prescott, where we had a summer cabin. We said we would stay there until we could decide what to do next. Winter was coming and a great deal had to be done to the cabin to get it ready for winter weather. Tom had never known what it was to be really tired. Always, after a hard day's work, he would say, "I am just healthfully tired." He went to the cabin alone, worked nonstop, and then collapsed!

For five days Tom was in the hospital. He was not sick; all he needed was complete rest. He had learned a good lesson. After his release, he hired help for the cabin and did not try to do it all by himself.

At last we were able to move in! A friend from our congregation came to hang our drapes, and as she worked she talked about the home on the hill. Her mother was a resident there, and she thought the place was great.

I had always known that home was there. I had known one person who had been a resident many years before, but I had not thought about the home for many years. Living there had never crossed my mind, but it required several days for the friend to finish the drapes, and she kept urging us to apply.

Us? Live in an "old people's home"? I couldn't imagine it, nor could Tom! We tried to be courteous but we were not interested.

Since the friend insisted that we look into it, we began asking other people what they thought. The pastor recommended the home highly and said he had never heard a word against it.

Although our friend kept saying, "Better get in before you get sick," we continued to assume that we wouldn't have any more health problems—really serious ones, I mean—at least for a few more years. There was no hurry. However, we did get brochures, and considered it a vague possibility for the future. We telephoned our girls and discussed the situation with them.

One night I was awakened suddenly out of a sound sleep, as if someone were saying, "Get up and work out that financial sheet." I felt it had to be the Lord speaking. The nudge was so strong that I got up and did it. In the morning I called the home and talked to the secretary, whom I had already met. "Send it in," she said, and it was done. I dismissed the matter from my mind.

A few days later we had a letter saying we had been accepted! Enter an "old folks' home"? We were in the midst of planning a "go-around" visit of our relatives! I talked to the secretary about that. "Take your trip," she replied. "When you return, call us."

Before I talked to her again, we visited all our children and grandchildren, several other family members, and a few friends. Tom had picked up a "bug" on the trip and was in the hospital for nine days. After that it wasn't much trouble to decide to enter the home as soon as they had another opening.

It took us a whole year to become fully adjusted to the home. Now we are both happy and content, and we love it fully. We feel sure the Lord led us here—against our will, perhaps—but we are positive now that we couldn't have made a better choice.

2

Where to Next?

When most people retire, they are in fairly good health. They are tired of the old grind and glad to change the pace. Usually in their 60s, they are and have been making plans for a long time. If they have been fortunate and thrifty, they have some savings. Their modest home is paid for; their funeral plots have been arranged for, long ago; they have had a few vacation trips along the way (maybe nothing big, but some); and they look forward to fulfilling various dreams.

Then they take a hard look at what inflation has done to their dreams. They think seriously about the cost of travel. They choose among the dreams and decide what they want to do most. Sometimes they decide the dreams are unattainable. One woman I used to know bought books all through the years, thinking she would have time to read when she retired. Alas, her eyes were almost gone by that time, and so the books remained unread.

Some dreams are unrealistic. A man went to the YMCA when he retired. I didn't know his plans but maybe he thought he would get his body in top condition in order to regain his youth or to enjoy sports. One day while he was playing ball at the Y, he had a heart attack. He was gone before they could get him to a hospital.

Another individual had been a professional ball player and had to quit playing because of his heart. He became a teacher and coach in an elementary school. One day he happened to be at one end of the gym when the basketball rolled from the other end to his feet. He picked it up and listened to the old urge to throw a basket right from there. He did. The ball went through the hoop perfectly, but he had a heart attack and was buried within a few days.

So many plans of "mice and men" go all awry. On the other hand, many people have stumbled upon success after retirement. Grandma Moses and Colonel Sanders have become legends! Occasionally we read of someone who wrote a successful first book at 80. Recently I saw on television that a minister in the Northeast had bought a farm home after he retired. It was way up in the mountains and he had thought it was for relaxation. His alert mind, however, discovered two worthwhile waterfalls on the place and, challenged by the energy crunch, he decided to make use of them. He educated himself and created an electrical plant which serviced not only his own home, but also a small community nearby. He found a new challenge and a new income as well as comfort!

Another minister, at retirement age, found himself alone. His wife had died, and he had little saved because he had always pastored struggling churches. He knew he would have to leave his present church soon. But what should he do? A young woman in the church appealed to him, and they married. She was only 19 and he was in his 60s. The congregation was outraged. The criticism was so bitter, they moved away.

All through his struggling years as a pastor and father,

this man had had a secret desire to run a store. He tried a small place but it was not a success. He and his young wife spent much time in prayer for guidance. They moved to Gila Bend, Ariz., and started another store. They promised the Lord that if He would direct and prosper them, they would give all their surplus to the work of the church, especially to missions.

Their prayers were abundantly answered. They gave large sums to missions, keeping separate account of how they disbursed the Lord's money, and they did many good deeds. Their store expanded and they hired help. As he grew older, she grew sharper and sharper in the business, until she was handling all of it. When he died, she handled everything beautifully. The store is a strong influence for good in that town. She is about to marry a man more nearly her own age, but he is not intending to tell her how to run her store!

A third minister started nine churches after he retired!

During the first two years of Tom's retirement, he took on the maintenance of the local church. He was already teaching a Bible class, serving as treasurer of the church, and as Sunday School superintendent! Nevertheless, he felt he wanted to clean the church each week, inside and out, and to mow the lawn. Occasionally, he also trimmed the shrubs and trees.

All his life Tom had worked largely at dairy farming but underneath had been an aptitude for building. So, one day, when a woman who lived near where I was teaching wanted someone to do some building for her, Tom went to see her. He built three houses for her. Later he helped in a subdivision building on 44 more houses. Eventually, he built our cabin at Prescott. All these things after retirement!

One couple we know wanted to combine travel and service, so they inquired of district superintendents of the church to locate struggling pastors and, traveling in a camper, spent three years helping these pastors both by physical labor and offerings. And what fun they had while they did it!

In the final analysis, each person must follow his own inclinations, multiply them by prayer, and accept the opportunities that present themselves.

3

Contentment

Contentment is a state of mind. The earlier in life we learn it, the better off we are. Contentment does not depend upon circumstances. If a person is discontented, it is usually because he is in the *habit* of finding fault with everything about him.

In 1 Tim. 6:5-6, Paul discusses this very subject. "Some men . . . suppose that *gain is godliness;* from such turn away. But *godliness with contentment* is great gain" (author's paraphrase).

In Phil. 4:11, he says, ". . . for I have *learned,* in *whatsoever state I am,* therewith to be content."

No one living can have everything he wants all the time, in every particular. Neither wealth, nor youth, nor pleasure, nor anything else can keep a human being content every moment of the day. We must use our common sense, and accept what we can't change!

Through my life I noticed that I was always content wherever I had a job teaching. Nothing else was important. The scenery, the environment, the housing, nothing was important. Only my job was significant. When the time came that I couldn't teach, I turned to writing. I had dozens of rejection slips, but if I could just sell one item now and then, I was content. I would write again.

By and large, it seems men have more difficulty being content than do women. To some men, retirement is a direct blow to the male ego. All their lives they have been in charge, they have been needed, they have provided for their families by going off to work. They feel lost, wandering about with nowhere to go. Sometimes there is a feeling of being in the way, especially for those whose new life centers around the house.

Women seem, more often than not, to have some special skill with a needle or find contentment with other lifelong hobbies. Men have to look about for a hobby. One man, who had been a mechanic all his life, chose a pattern for making decorative windmills for the front yard. The little mills were attractive, and many were sold. Soon he had found a source for pin money as well as a hobby to fill in his time.

One man here in the home carried his outside work on by making clever necklaces and bolo ties after he came to the home. He was 95 when I knew him, so his jewelry was out of style. Even at that he still sold a tie now and then and his self-entertainment had lasted for several years.

Another, whom I knew in his active years, always kept books in strategic places, so any time he had to wait for something or someone, he picked up the book closest to him and read a few pages. It was said of Henry Ford, Sr., that after he was no longer doing the heavy work in his great company, he had a Bible in each strategic place, where he might sit and read a bit.

A relative of mine commuted from Pasadena to Los Angeles regularly. She was secretary in an insurance firm. She had a basket of crochet work (or maybe knitting), which she carried on the interurban, and filled the two hours of transportation time doing profitable work. At her desk, she had a simpler bit of crochet, which she kept in the bottom drawer. When the work was slack, she would do a few stitches (though of course she tried not to allow clients to catch her).

At her adorable little home tucked away in some hills, she had another basket of more intricate work, which she did under better light, when she had ample time. But, biggest of all, at her widowed mother's home, on weekends, she had hooked rug equipment. Here she did the most beautiful of all her work. Oh, how pretty the rugs were! Unfortunately, she did not live to retirement age, but she certainly had her hobbies well mapped out!

It is a sad thing when a person reaches maturity without having mastered the art of keeping content. If one can't accept his lot in life when he is healthy and active, he will be quite a problem to everyone around him when his day of uncertain health arrives.

Pitiful is the person—and oh, how miserable!—who cannot be pleased with *anything*. I know people who are never satisfied with the food, the service, the roommate, or who are ready to take offense at any and every thing that is said to him or her! Pitiful is the person who sits in the lobby all day criticizing everyone in sight. Old age has enough strains on one's emotions without the handicap of a critical attitude. How well I know! It is very difficult to keep even a semblance of patience when you have to have help for every paragraph you read, or for each tiny seam you need to repair. Bad eyes can make one cross!

However, the people who have severe hearing loss have just as much frustration. They can't hear announcements, can't hear the TV, can't hear a sermon or good music. Many can get some help from hearing aids, but practically everyone must learn endurance.

Afflictions are a part of the package of growing old and *great* is the person who can cope graciously! When we must keep on living, we have no choice but to pray much and put forth extra effort to stay pleasant. Those caring for us have their problems, too!

4

Money

The Bible tells us that the love of money is the root of all evil; but it also says that we should be diligent in business, fervent in spirit, serving the Lord. Again, it tells us that if we give, it shall be given to us! Now somewhere among these three concepts must lie a balanced way of handling money: being thrifty, but not stingy; being careful and wise, without being crafty or covetous. At least, we can try!

In addition to these scriptures are some old clichés that bear sound advice. "If you have money, you have friends." "When poverty comes in the door, love files out the window." "If you lend money to a friend, he becomes your enemy." "If you accept money from a friend, you are forever indebted to him." No doubt there are others.

I read of a farmer whose reputation for getting along with his employees was indeed fabulous. His rule was that every agreement he and his men made on the day of employment was written down on paper. No one signed anything, but each man kept a copy in his files. Then when an argument threatened to arise, each would go back to the written agreement, and be satisfied. Therefore the threat would be dissipated, with harmony restored instantly.

It seems to me that dealing with family and friends

could be handled in a similar manner, and thus no serious problems with money would arise. We borrowed money from my father one time to buy cows. He handed us a note saying, "I would never take you to court, but I want you and Tom both to sign this note." We did. Later we paid every penny back. Thus we established credit with him. When there is no understanding between relatives or friends, there are reservations, suspicions, and doubts, and finally just plain enmity. People have to establish a "square-dealing" relationship between each other, if there is to be happiness and good feeling. By the same token, *nothing* destroys fellowship among relatives like careless or indifferent handling of money.

There is also nothing that upsets elderly parents so much, or so quickly or permanently toward children as the childish attitude of adult young people toward the tired, worn, and frugal parent. Bitterness will consume one or the other if great care is not taken.

On the other hand, a lifelong friend of mine told me after her widowed mother passed away, "I always wished my mother had been willing to help us when we were struggling to raise our six children. She left us money when she passed away—but we didn't need it then! I still ache over that."

Another family I knew about felt that their mother helped the youngest son more than was good for him, which was unfair to the other family members. It simply is not easy to walk the perfect line between all members of a household!

Still another family had a mute son. All effort was made to give this son a full and complete education. As a result, he became reasonably wealthy, while the normal children had to manage the best they could alone, and none of them did very well. They felt cheated!

After the funeral of a certain widow, her relatives went to gather up her belongings and dispose of them, while a neighbor had stood by the lady faithfully all during her illness and death. The poor lady had no money to give the neighbor but she did tell her she could have two pieces of her furniture. The neighbor explained to the young relatives—who scarcely knew the great-aunt—what she had done and what agreement had been reached. The young people however, didn't believe the neighbor. They felt she was only being grabby, so they ignored her. How much bitterness must have come to the helpful neighbor. If only the agreement had been written down with maybe another neighbor to witness—the problem could have been resolved satisfactorily.

An old man, alone and unattached, knew he was dying. He wrote a letter to his brother, and told him he wanted the brother to have his watch. Meanwhile, a woman called on him occasionally. One day she picked up the watch and took it home with her. A friend told the brother what had happened. When he went to investigate, the woman said, "He owed me for a board bill, so I took the watch." Maybe that was true, and maybe it wasn't. Nobody knew. But she kept the watch!

The son of a minister died, leaving a large family mostly without funds. His brother, another son of the same minister, died. In his will it was provided that at the passing of his widow, the entire estate should be divided equally among all the children of the two families. All the people involved knew of the will. They had even seen it. But when the mother passed away, one daughter took the will, changed the name to herself, and took the entire property. They could have taken it to court, but a member of the defrauded family said, "I wouldn't have brought that disgrace to my husband's memory, for any amount of money!" In other words, "Vengeance is mine; I will repay, saith the Lord" (Rom. 12:19).

Such stories can be multiplied on and on. However, one more comes to mind. A widower lived alone. His daughter kept writing that she was coming to see him. First it was June; then in September; then it was Thanksgiving; later it was Christmas; but not one time did she get there. Eventually another family member began writing, assuring the old man how much they loved and cared for him . . . He must come and live with them and spend the rest of his days with his own people. He sold out, and went. He had scarcely arrived until he learned that they had overextended themselves in remodeling their home, and were about to lose it. They wanted his money to bail them out of debt! He didn't accept the offer! He went back to the town whence he had come, went into a rest home, and spent his money there!

One man we knew personally, lost his wife. He couldn't sell his nice home quickly enough. He couldn't stand the empty house. A cousin in Texas had insisted that he come there to live. He went. In almost nothing flat, he was back and trying desperately to buy his home back; but had no luck. He did not say WHY he came back, but he never could regain his home. I do not know what he did, but the moral is: "Don't be too quick to make changes."

True, you can't take your money with you. True, it would be nice or even glamorous to be philanthropic, to give large chunks to close relatives, to the church, or whatever, but you never know how long you may have to live. You should be as thrifty in old age as when you were younger.

Wills are a necessity, and should be made by a qualified lawyer to avoid as many squabbles as possible. A lady here in the home who was a secretary for a lawyer for nine years said it was amazing how many quarrels and court battles came up over money; and so often with people who *seemed* to be the finest of the fine!

A story is told of a prominent man in Phoenix. I would not attempt to prove or disprove the story, but it goes like this: The man was the founder of a large bank. He had been a brilliant, capable, and successful man. But in time his children declared him incompetent; put him in a rest home, and left him there without money and without friends. They never came to see him.

Even if the children did the right thing knowing it was not safe for him to handle large sums of money any more, it seems to me that they could have set up a small account for him just to keep his ego from being completely destroyed! Above all, they should have let him know they still cared. He was so alone and felt so lost.

In another situation, an old lady was living alone with a great-niece and husband living 100 miles or more away, her only relatives in the Western states. They voluntarily assumed the responsibility of checking on her every so often, increasing the frequency of their visits as she grew more feeble. They repaired the little house; did some of the heavy cleaning; mowed the lawn; and bought groceries. She appreciated what they did and grew to trust them fully. She gave legal permission for them to cash her checks, so they could pay her bills, so she didn't need to go to town. One day she told them she had made her will to them. The house and lot were to be theirs, for the services rendered. They had not expected this but were grateful. Then one day she became miffed over some triffle and told them she had changed her will. She was leaving the property to another great-niece over on the East coast, one she had never seen!

These faithful young people could have said, "Well,

if you feel like that you just send for this perfect niece and let her take over here for you." But they didn't. They were strong Christians and stayed put, just as usual. The aunt died and they made the funeral arrangements. There were a few dollars left in the bank and they took that; and so far as I know, they never did see the other niece!

My mother had a distant relative in Arizona, where we visited a time or two. She had several sons, all but one of whom were helpful and considerate. To the delinquent son, she said one day, "Jeb, do you see this pair of salt and pepper shakers?" "Yes, Ma." "Well, that is the only thing you have ever given me for Christmas—or any other time. I want you to know that those shakers are the only thing you will inherit from me!"

We smiled, of course, but we always wondered how it came out. Did the son change his ways, or did she actually carry out her threat?

Some people have found that having secrets in the family makes for doubts and reservations, if not outright misunderstandings. Everyone responds much better if there is openness, in money deals, especially.

After we have done our best to keep peace with all involved, and still fail; we can just lean a little harder on the tenth commandment and "Covet NOT." Leave it all with the Lord, for the closer we get to the end of the journey, the less these things mean to us anyway.

One final story will close this section of the contemplation of the wrap-up years. A dear lady of ancient vintage told me her experience during the Great Depression of the 30s.

They had a neighborhood grocery, and they had a large family. During this period of time, money became almost nonexistent. People had nothing with which to buy groceries. Her husband could not bear to see people go hungry, so he let them charge. At the end of seven years, he died. After the funeral, the banker came to her and said, "Come to the bank; I have to see you." When she went he showed her just how much they owed the wholesalers for groceries! The amount was hopelessly large. He said, "I'll do anything I can to help you." She said, "What do you suggest?" He said, "You can take out bankruptcy." "No," she answered and went back to the store.

There would be no time to grieve. She didn't know what to do, but she did know she had to sell groceries and no more charging. She was a woman of prayer, so her spare time was spent that way.

Two sons-in-law got their heads together and wrote a letter to this burdened woman. "Do not expect us to help with the store, and don't expect our wives to help either." (Who knows? maybe they thought she should have gone into bankruptcy.) When she received that letter, she was stunned. Her reply was simple: "Why didn't you wait until you were asked?"

By contrast, another son-in-law, Jewish by faith, supported her faithfully and completely. He did anything and everything he could do to help her. He did not work in the store but offered support and advice. While he worked in his way, she prayed in her way. After five years, she had every debt paid. Over and over she hoped and prayed that those whom they had helped during the great crisis would come forth and pay what they owed. No one ever did!

How easily this woman could have gone into bitterness with a capital "B." But she prayed her way through that, too. However, she does have one climactic thing to say, "My Jewish son-in-law was better than my son. He was better than 10 sons!"

5

What You <u>Believe</u> Influences Everything You <u>Do</u>

If you don't believe in a hereafter, you convince yourself that nothing here matters. You can do as you please, and you die just like any other animal. If you believe in the transmigration of the soul, you may hope you will come back as one far better than you are now. If you believe in a long sleep, you have no concept of a homegoing. Which reminds me:

Once I was invited to visit a very sick woman of another faith. She was badly crippled with arthritis. As she lay there in her clean white bed, my heart went out to her. Considering her condition she was the most cheerful person I had ever seen. I chatted with her for a few minutes, enjoying her sparkling replies but aching for her suffering. I felt sure she must be really anxious to have it all over with. After a bit of conversation, I asked if she would like us to pray a bit. She consented. Nazarene me, I dropped to my knees beside her bed and prayed like this: "Lord, bless this precious one. Thou seest her suffering; please give her a great homegoing."

I felt my prayer was hitting a stone wall. I looked up and she was watching me. Very courteously she said, "We don't believe in a homegoing. We believe in a long sleep until the Day of Judgment."

I was stunned! I had never heard of such a thing. I had no answer. She was much too ill to offer any kind of an argument, so I slipped away at once. I never saw her again but I have often wondered what she actually found when she passed away. Believe me, I sorrowed more than ever for her.

I fully believe in a homegoing and truly expect to have one! If the Christ, or one of His messengers, meets me at the gate of death, I shall *not* be afraid. I shall be gloriously happy and make the transition with rejoicing.

If I thought for one minute that He would *not* be there, I would certainly then be *afraid.* My belief is what keeps me from having fear. There are many things in the wrap-up years that cause apprehension—such as finances, children, differences in faith, even among your own loved ones; doubts of in-laws; who will care for you when you are beyond your own ability. Many things can disturb. I have tried to cover most of them.

In this section, I want to tell how I feel about the closing moments, or hours.

Some years ago a nurse told me her experience. She said that in all her years of working she had never seen but one person afraid at death. That was a man so full of bitterness that he fought terribly at the last. In her experience, most people went peacefully.

When I was in Pasadena College, working my way through school, I overdid and had a bad time with nervous exhaustion. I was placed in the infirmary there. Much prayer was made for me in the chapel, and nurses came and went in my room. As for me, I felt I was nearly gone; but, if I would turn my head toward the wall, I could see Jesus. His face was in a circle of gold, like a picture frame.

If I turned away, I'd lose Him; so I kept my face constantly in that position. It was so comforting to see Him, and that memory is just as vivid today as it was 60 years ago. After I was better, someone told me that one nurse felt the presence of angels every time she entered that room. It was a thrilling comment to hear, but I never did see or feel the angels—only the Christ.

Years later I was teaching in Bethany High School and my husband was working his way through college by milking cows and pedaling milk in the town. We had a student living in our home, helping with the kitchen work. All three of us worked hard, I at washing bottles and filling them with milk, the girl washing dishes and pans. One Saturday my work load was exceedingly heavy. I had done the family washing, cleaned the house; our three-year-old and I had had our bath and shampooed our hair: I knew I was too tired to do even one more thing. I was about to go to bed, when the telephone rang.

The voice of Tom's sister's neighbor came over the wire. "Mrs. Verner, little Barbara has been vomiting all night, and until now. Nell has been up all this time. I've been over there much of today. Would you come help so Nell can go to bed?"

I ask you: "How would you turn down a request like that?" I couldn't, of course. Tom took me over, and I held the sweet baby in my arms and put cold compresses on her throat. Nell went to bed, and I took over. Tom went back to wash bottles and get the milking done. He would have to do it all alone this time. He said he'd get back as soon as possible. The compresses had to be changed every few minutes. When he did get back, he took the baby and let me rest a bit. She just didn't get better. All night we worked, and at five in the morning we called Nell.

We went home and the milking routine began all over

again. When we had finished, it was time to go to Sunday School. I began to get ready, but fever and chills shook me. I knew I couldn't stay up, so I dressed for bed.

Tom offered to call the doctor, but I told him I knew I was just too tired. Then he said he would stay home with me. I said, "No, it will be better if you take the baby and go on and leave the house completely quiet. I just need to rest." He did.

Sooner than I can say, I was at "the river." I felt the Christ near the foot of my bed. I was "aware" of angels swaying or teetering, at the head of my bed. Suddenly it dawned upon me, "This is death!" The angels are here to take me over, but Christ hasn't given permission yet." Then it struck me: "My life is accepted!" It was such a marvelous revelation that I said it again, "*My* life is accepted!" Immediately I thought of my unsaved brother and wished I could leave a testimony. Next I said, "Tom will be a better father than I am a mother, so our daughter will be all right!" I could feel the celestial breezes from across the river pulling me over. I have never been able to find words to describe those breezes! My, but I wanted to go!

Afterward, I felt sleepy, but I was afraid to go to sleep, fearful I might not wake up. Immediately it occurred to me: "Jesus is here. If I don't wake up, it will be all right." So I relaxed.

The next thing I knew, Tom and the baby were coming in the driveway. My first impulse was to say nothing; it would only disturb him. I remembered I had wanted to leave a testimony. Perhaps this was my opportunity. I was in no way able to get out of bed, but I told him. He began to weep, and said he would get the doctor. The doctor came and said, "I could give you a stimulant, but it would be like whipping a tired horse. You just can't burn the candle at both ends. Stay in bed the whole week; then maybe you'll be able to teach next week."

What happened after that is not important. What *is* important is that, after almost 53 years, the memory is almost as vivid as it was that day. And I have never been deeply afraid of death since.

I did have a bit of fear once, though, when my third child was an infant. I realized that, for some unknown reason, I was not doing as well as I should, and suddenly I began to have fear. Instantly, down through the roof came an angelic figure and stood by my bed. I did not *see* him, because the veil was there, but I was aware of him, and I knew at once that I was going to be all right. That, too, is still vivid.

I have never sought to have any of these experiences; I wouldn't dare! But one more might be profitable. We were living in Pasadena again, after our daughters were half grown. In the missionary society, the women had decided to spend a dollar each, to see how much money we could make through the use of our talents. The money, of course, was to go to missions.

Well, some of them baked things, and sold them by the slice, which multiplied their dollar. I was a writer of sorts, so I put together a memorial card for my mother who had not been gone for very long. I had it printed. One day I was driving down Colorado Street going to pick up my cards at the printer, and start selling them. Suddenly I was aware of my mother floating beside the car, in flowing white. I *saw* her!

"Do not do this," she said.

"Mamma, I have to get my money back, before there is anything to give."

She said no more, but floated away. I became stunned.

"Lord," I said. *"That* was *my mother*—and she is

33

dead." I repeated it. "That was *my mother!* and she is dead!" "Thank You for letting her talk to me. O Lord, I thank You so much!"

I paid for the cards, and showed them at the Society—but I made no effort to sell them. I didn't understand why she did not want me to make a profit for the Lord, but I obeyed her, just the same. The project, so far as I was concerned, was a flop. I have a few of those cards still.

I saw my father once also, and he, too warned me about money. Since then, I have been almost afraid of money—more afraid of it than of death!

"Though I walk through the valley of the shadow of death, I will fear no evil: for thou art with me" (Ps. 23:4).

6

How Others See
the Wrap-up Years

In order to get the reactions of other people who are retired, it was suggested that I make a questionnaire and get people to express themselves.

Some of the people I contacted felt that no one should know their business, and they refused to contribute. Others said, "I'll say something, but don't use my name!" Their requests have been respected. But quite a few were happy to give us their ideas and experiences. All these names have been listed alphabetically. Much has been gained from their willingness to be included.

My appreciation is expressed herewith! It was most kind of them to take this interest, and I hope something they have said will encourage you in *your* wrap-up years!

ALBERT E. AND LOUISE BEEKER

This is a beautiful response to our questionnaire! These people were in their 60s when they retired. They sold their home, bought a 35-foot mobile home and truck, and started out to explore America. Louise wrote:

> We left California in August, 1979. Our first stop was Prescott, Ariz., to attend the Nazarene camp meeting; also to see our former neighbors and friends, Annalee and Gene Meister.

Plans were to spend a few months in a warm climate, then travel to Michigan and, hopefully, into the New England States in early fall, 1980. After that we wanted to go to Florida for the winter of 1980-81.

The camp meeting was a real blessing and it was good to meet many of our friends. After staying on the campgrounds for a few weeks, we saw the need for workers. We dropped our travel plans. With God's leading we stayed in Prescott and lived in our trailer. It was a wonderful experience in many ways. Mr. Beeker felt he could do something for the Lord by helping to repair buildings; he even got to be a good cook's-helper, dish washer, and pie sampler. He loved it and many times his remark was, "I'm so thankful to be useful for the Lord." God always has work for a good carpenter and worker, and we know that's true.

I kept busy, too, helping in the kitchen, office, and elsewhere. Knowing we were where God wanted us, along with His blessings and meeting former friends, and making so many new friends, we are loved and our prayer is that we can give more love to others.

Due to Mr. Beeker's illness in May, followed by surgery in June, we are now living in a mobile home. We are happy here in Prescott, and trust God will let us live our remaining days here. We love to fish, go camping and work.

To help some new retirees to become adjusted to the future, we would say: make plans and goals, but let God lead you. Most of all, keep busy, and make each day count something for Christ and His work. Plan to have a time to yourselves each day; especially the wife needs time to do her usual housework. Keep the days going smoothly.

We have no fears. None of us likes to face getting

older but I feel God can help us to grow sweeter and to love more. He is still able to take care of us *daily*.

For scripture, we would mention Psalm 23 and Psalm 37. Don't fret. There are songs which are a real blessing and a comfort: "Jesus Never Fails" and "Let's Just Praise the Lord."

H. H. AND MARILYN BOLTON

They retired earlier than most because of health reasons: a heart attack for him; eye problems for her. They are wonderful people and very talented. They have traveled some, but believe in exploring the things nearby that do not require heavy expense.

Their advice to new retirees is:

Be sure you have a hobby or two to keep you interested. Keep interested in people, your church, and your community. Keep meeting *new* friends of all ages. Plan ahead!

I can't think of any fear except that of displeasing the Lord. Death is God's way of taking me to be with Him.

"Let not your heart be troubled, neither let it be afraid. . . . I go to prepare a place for you. . . . I will come again, and receive you unto myself; that where I am, there ye may be also" (John 14:27, 2-3).

MATTIE CONWAY

She wrote in her questionnaire:

I was in my early 70s when I retired. For 30 years I had been housekeeper at Judson School in Scottsdale, Ariz. I went there in 1932 when Mr. Judson owned the school.

My idea for retirement is to live one day at a time. Treat other people as you want to be treated.

I have no fears; I do have many scripture promises.

KEN AND GERRY DUNN

They retired at 60. They sold their condominium in California and moved to Arizona. They fell in love with the gorgeous scenery, found an adorable home just being completed, facing those wonderful rocks, and bought it! "Next we opened a gift shop downtown, which had been a long dream of our youngest son. This shop has been a splendid success and has been a delightful place for us, the parents, to keep busy showing and selling what our son and others create. Gerry feared loneliness, at first; but soon these fears faded as she put her zest and enthusiasm into the life of the community.

Gerry writes:

As to death, I am not afraid of tomorrow; I have had yesterday, and I *love* today! Psalm 23 is my special scripture.

Ken's testimony:

Since we are living in such a busy-busy, rush-rush day and age, I am enjoying my retirement particularly in my daily devotions and prayer life. I like to study special topics, hunting up scriptures on those lines. I find much more time to be thankful, to look for the needs of others and pray for them.

I'm also seeking to find the will of God for my very "old age." I feel surely there is something special for me, be it ever so small. God bless this book!

STANLEY AND VIOLA GIRDNER

This couple retired early and has not regretted it:

We joined the Christian Endeavor, and have found fulfillment.

I suggest to others to apply themselves to the teaching of the Bible, for their complete fulfillment for this life and to prepare for the next. We have too many favorite scriptures to list here.

One man we knew said he was not afraid to die, but he surely would hate to miss all those retirement checks he'd be losing!

KEN JOHNSON

I retired in early 60s and came to Arizona where my health improved about 75 percent. I went into a small business which provided a modest income.

My one fear is for my wife's future. She is 30 years younger than I am, so Social Security is a long way off for her. I know she could not support herself with the small wage she earns in day-care. I find myself worrying about how she would get along without my check.

I consider death a change for the better, not the end. The scripture which applies to me is Job 14:14: "All the years of my appointed time will I wait, till my change come."

EVA KAU

The special thing that I did for my family was to dedicate our lives to the Lord. As each child was loaned to us, we had great responsibility in shaping and guiding their lives. As each child confessed Jesus as Lord and Savior, it became our greatest joy to help him grow in grace and in service. Each one has taken a special place in God's field, from the eldest to the youngest.

To help new retirees to become adjusted, I would say that, several years before coming to the Poineers' Home, I took into my home children from broken homes, and also elderly folks who needed help. These things I did after my daughter and three sons were married. My husband's death came so suddenly and there were many responsibilities.

The thought of death does not frighten me. I have no fears because I cast my problems on my Lord: 1 Pet. 5:4.

God's promises for daily living are so many that I am more concerned about that, and about giving Him the praise.

M. L. MANN

I retired at 66. We moved to Prescott into our own home. I was a pastor, so the Arizona District gave us a "retirement gift" which enabled us to pay off the mortgage on the house and on our car. This permitted us to leave the center of activity and yet remain in Arizona, close to our children and our many friends.

We did some traveling, and I requested an evangelist's commission which made it possible for me to hold a number of revival campaigns.

It is important for a retiree to look at his or her new relationship in a positive way. We are not "demoted," but have completed an era of our lives with distinction. Now we are free to choose a pattern of activity or leisure with great flexibility. Indeed, there are far more options now open to us than ever before.

I have no fears. A concern would be a major

disease which would prevent me from pursuing a normally active role in life. I would not want to be bedridden or seriously confined until I came to be dependent upon others. I am not afraid of death.

When we contemplated serving Christ nearly 50 years ago, the promise of Matt. 6:33 was made so real that it has been our lode-star ever since. Matthew 28:20, with John 14:1-3, is all we need as we come to the wrap-up years of our lives. "It will be worth it all when we see Jesus."

JANE MEYER

I retired at 65. We sold our home in California. My husband was a plumber but had a brain hemorrhage and could no longer continue in that work. The children were all gone, so we sold the nearly new home and bought a travel trailer and a better car. This took a large share of the money from the sale of the home, which had been mortgaged. We both wanted to live in Arizona, but took a trip to the Northwest first. We spent one winter in Phoenix, and needed some income. I worked for the state in Yuma, and my husband found work as a bookkeeper. We could then save some of our salaries.

I have no fears about the future. I feel secure, in a worldly sense, in having this home and its security. I have no fears for the hereafter because of the many promises in the Bible, which I believe to be the Word of God.

I am not frightened by the thought of death. I have the promise of eternal life, and believe it.

There are too many promises to list, but one comes to mind often, from Proverbs: "Trust in the

Lord with all thine heart; and lean not unto thine own understanding. In *all* thy ways acknowledge him, and he shall direct thy paths."

Doris Mylott

This wonderful woman retired at 61, but she kept busy by assisting a disabled sister in a nursing home, keeping house, and taking care of an aging mother. She still had time to serve as volunteer driver for people who needed transportation, and she took classes at Yavapai College in lip reading, water color, and cultural courses.

Doris believes that new retirees should plan for retirement, looking forward to it as a new adventure.

She advises:

> Be mentally prepared to make some changes in life-style. Try to become involved in a community activity. Get outside of yourself.
>
> There are fears in wondering if my finances will last as long as I will live, and will my mind be stable? In order to cope with these I try to live one day at a time, and be thankful for today and what I have.
>
> Death is inevitable; it is something to be accepted. The unknown is always frightening. I find these words from "Lead Kindly Light" a comforting thought: "So long Thy power has blessed me, sure it still will lead me on."

Mary Sarvis

Retired at 71, Mary Sarvis moved from Michigan to Arizona in 1945. Her advice to new retirees is:

> Get your things in order, such as your will, finances, insurance, etc. Establish your residence for

the rest of your days, with peace of mind and no responsibilities.

As to fears, she says:

I fear lightning. I adjust myself to it, and let God do the rest. The thought of death does not frighten me. I believe it is something good to look forward to, everlasting life in heaven; with no more problems.

O. Schopp

This lovely lady retired in her early 60s. Her husband died, and she remarried. Fifteen years ago she had a stroke which left her right arm and hand completely paralyzed. The left leg is badly damaged, also. She does get around, though, is never sick, and has no pain. She is always cheerful, never complaining. She is just a beautiful person. She says she has no fears and her favorite scripture is, "The Lord is my shepherd; I shall not want."

Curtis and Wife Scurlock

Mr. Scurlock became disabled and retired at 62. His wife writes:

We sold our small farm and took a trailer as down payment. The trailer was at Phoenix, so we moved there. Because of the intense heat, we spent our summers on my sister's farm in McLean, Tex. We lived in Phoenix for five years. We felt we had it made, because the trailer was near a grocery store, a bank, and a drug store. But Curt would climb when needed, and that kept me uneasy. I had a heart condition, so we decided to move into a home where we could be cared for. We can't begin to count our blessings here.

We are born-again Christians, so we shall not be

frightened at death, we just dread the parting with our loved ones.

Curt's hobby is music. Mine is art and reading.

Mr. Scurlock has some very fine stereo equipment, obtained in his active years. Daily he brings this equipment up the elevator to the lobby and plays records from his enormous collection, for the people relaxing there. This is a wonderful service, indeed, and is greatly appreciated.

GLEN J. SOWERS

He retired from Sears at 60 and has been on call for odd jobs ever since. These include handy-man work, such as plumbing, electrical repairs, etc., most of which he did while working in the appliance department of the store.

He says:

My advice is to associate with good people; have a hobby; keep busy. My fears had to do with family problems, security, etc. Trusting in the Lord is the key for coping, I think. He does make changes for us! My favorite scriptures are found in John 14 and 2 Thessalonians.

MR. AND MRS. RICHARD C. TABLER

My wife and I ran the Prescott Transfer and Storage Co. for 21 years. Then we sold out, and I worked for the Santa Fe Railroad until 1958. I retired in middle 60s. We traveled some and I had a hobby of making small windmills.

My advice to others is to find a hobby, and take it easy! My one fear is sickness. My way of coping is through prayer for healing.

Gail and Donna Taken

I retired at 65, and for two years I had a part-time job. One year after that, we sold out and moved from Iowa to Arizona. We had no problem adjusting to retirement. Hobbies, travel, part-time employment, and "exploring" the Prescott area have kept us busy.

Death itself does not frighten me, but I do dread the infirmities of old age! My favorite scriptures are Heb. 13:5 and John 14:2-3.

Vada Vaughn

This lady is a wonderful Christian person. She has passed her 89th birthday and still helps in the dining room. Often the powers that be have urged her to quit, but she begs to be permitted to help. She loves the home and can't bear to hear any criticism of it!

She says:

I came here after an auto accident. I am contented and grateful for wonderful care. I have encouraged my grandchildren to seek educational goals and have been gratified with the results.

I have many hobbies, and other interests, things I like to do and that I need to do to keep on living. I have a fear of falling, or accident. I am careful when I move about, and use a cane.

After Jesus rose from the dead, He told His disciples that He was going to prepare a place for them and all other believers. That is my comfort.

Edna Cole Wells

I retired from teaching when I was 70. I had saved a lot of books, and cut-out articles; I wrote some—I have a number of poems; I was active at church, and in community affairs. I even took a motherless child into my home. I did not go into business, as such, but there is always some business involved in the care of oneself, home, and community affairs. Several years later, I sold out and moved into the Arizona Pioneers' Home.

My advice to others is to trust in the Lord, keep busy, and do for others. My favorite verse is, "I am with you always" (Matt. 28:20).

Many other people added their thoughts on retirement years through unsigned testimonies. The advice contained in them might be helpful to someone, so let me pass it along in capsule form.

—one welcomed release from secretarial work to enjoy housework!
—one made up her mind the "home" was *home*, determining to be happy there.
—a couple with some physical problems plans into their schedule either traveling or college classes (and the husband, realizing the housewife doesn't get to retire, helps her with the work at home).

Death does not seem to be a fearsome enemy in the wrap-up years. Most of those I surveyed said they did not fear death, and one unsigned form explained it this way: "Death will be the end of the sufferings I have seen and a joyous reunion with the Lord and loved ones and friends." She crowned the testimonies with this beautiful comment: "I have never been so happy as in the last 15 years nor felt more rewarded. My advice to others is to seek and find the Lord's will and fellowship with His people . . . We must keep on serving the Lord!"

Finale

It would seem that people are most afraid of running out of money before they are actually called to go.

My father, at 86, was always afraid his funds would expire before he did. He was in the hospital and each evening he would insist that I go to the office and pay the bill up to date. I knew he had a margin—inflation hadn't taken over, at that time—I was embarrassed to do this, but I knew he would not sleep one wink if I didn't, so I did.

Fortunately, for all concerned, he was called on the 15th day of his stay. I had stepped out for a brief rest, and he seemed to know; for he called my husband by name, and said, "Everett, come stand right by me." My husband punched the buzzer as he came. Doctors and nurses came running, and someone called me. Whereas for days, it had been garbled, his voice was perfectly clear when he spoke. He gave no sign of fear, but we never knew whether or not he felt the presence of the Lord.

Others fear the long siege of helpless sickness. Who wouldn't? We had a lady here at the home who died the other day, after eight long years in the infirmary. Only God's grace could take a person through that ordeal. He would need a raft of scriptures in his heart to lean upon. There are many "fear nots" in the Bible, and I have chosen Isaiah 41:10 just for *me!*